WALKING IN LOVE

"And we have known and believed the love that God hath to us. God is love; and he that dwelleth in love dwelleth in God, and God in him."

1 John 4:16

by

Franklin N. Abazie

Walking In Love
COPYRIGHT 2017 BY Franklin N Abazie
ISBN: 978-1-945-133-83-1

All right reserved. This book or any portion thereof may not be reproduced or used in any manner whatsoever without the express written permission of the publisher, except for the use of brief quotations in a book review. All Bible quotes are from King James Version and others as noted.

Published by: F N ABAZIE PUBLISHING HOUSE- aka, Empowerment Bookstore.

That I may publish with the voice of thanksgiving and tell of all thy wondrous works.
Psalms 26:7

To order additional copies, wholesales
or booking:
Call the Church office (973-372-7518),
or Empowerment Bookstore Hotline (973-393-8518)

Worship address:
343 Sanford Avenue Newark New Jersey 07106
Administrative Head Office address:
33 Schley Street Newark New Jersey 07112
Email:pastorfranknto@yahoo.com
Website www.fnabaziehealingministries.org
Publishing House: www.fnabaziepublishinghouse.org

This book is a production of F N Abazie Publishing House.
A publication Arms of Miracle of God Ministries 2017.
First Edition

CONTENTS

THE MANDATE OF THE COMMISSION iv

ARMS OF THE COMMISSION v

INTRODUCTION vi

CHAPTER 1
1 What Is Love? 1

CHAPTER 2
2 How Do I Walk In Love? 10

CHAPTER 3
3 Prayer of Salvation 27

CHAPTER 4
4 About The Author 38

THE MANDATE OF THE COMMISSION

"THE MOMENT IS DUE TO IMPACT YOUR WORLD THROUGH THE REVIVAL OF THE HEALING & MIRACLE MINISTRY OF JESUS CHRIST OF NAZARETH."

"I AM SENDING YOU TO RESTORE HEALTH UNTO THEE AND I WILL HEAL THEE OF THY WOUNDS, SAID THE LORD OF HOST."

ARMS OF THE COMMISSION

1) F N Abazie Ministries-Miracle of God Ministries (Miracle Chapel Intl)

2) F N Abazie TV Ministries: Global Television Ministry Outreach

3) F N Abazie Radio Ministries: Radio Broadcasting Outreach

4) F N Abazie Publishing House: Book Publication

5) F N Abazie Bible School: also called Word of Healing Bible School (W.O.H.B.S)

6) F N Abazie Evangelistic Ass: Miracle of God Ministries: Global Crusade

7) Empowerment Bookstore: Book distribution

8) F N Abazie Helping Hands: Meeting the help of the needy world wide

9) F N Abazie Disaster Recovery Mission: Global Disaster Recovery

10) F N Abazie Prison Ministry: Prison Ministry for all convicts "Second chance"

Some of our ministry arms are waiting the appointed time to commence.

FAVOR CONFESSION

Father thank you for making me righteous and accepted through the blood of Jesus Christ. Because of that, I am blessed and highly favored by God. I am the subject of your affection. Your favor surrounds me as a shield, and the first thing that people see around me is your favored shield.

Thank you that I have favor with you and man today. All day long people go out of their way to bless me and help me. I have favor with everyone that I deal with today. Doors that were once closed are now opened for me. I receive preferential treatment, and I have special privileges, I am Gods favored child.

No good thing will he withhold from me. Because of Gods favor my enemies cannot triumph over my life. I have supernatural increase and promotion. I declare restoration to everything that the devil has stolen from my life. I have honor in the midst of my adversaries and an increase in assets, especially in real estate and expansion of territories.

Because I am highly favored by God, I experience great victories, supernatural turnarounds, and miraculous breakthrough in the midst of great impossibilities. I receive recognition, prominence, and honor. Petitions are granted to me even by ungodly authorities. Policies, rules, regulations, and laws are changed and reverse on my behalf.

I win battles that I don't even have to fight, because God fights them for me. This is the day, the set time and the designated moment for me to experience the free favor of God, that profusely and lavishly abound on my behalf in Jesus name. **Amen.**

INTRODUCTION

"And we have known and believed the love that God hath to us. God is love; and he that dwelleth in love dwelleth in God, and God in him." **1 John 4:16**

Although to love and be loved is the greatest existence of happiness, someone said. For anyone to *walk in love*, in my opinion, it is a choice we make from the heart. But for anyone to *walk in love*, they must repent of any bitterness inside of their heart. It is written, "For if ye forgive men their trespasses, your heavenly Father will also forgive you:

But if ye forgive not men their trespasses, neither will your Father forgive your trespasses." (Matthew 6:14-15) This publication is designed to help anyone live in forgiveness. It is a book that encourages everyone to live in peace and love.

Some of us just want to dwell in regret, reflect only on failure and what didn't work out for them. Others chose to live in bitterness, and live in malice, hatred, resentment, and envy. Every time you live in malice, jealousy, and bitterness you can never go forward in life. This publication is a book to help anyone live in love, celebrate our liberty in Christ, and look forward to a great future in life. It is written, *"For God so loved the world, that he gave his only begotten*

Son, that whosoever believeth in him should not perish, but have everlasting life." **John 3:16**

This publication is a *hand manual to help you walk in love* the remaining days of your life. *"But as it is written, Eye hath not seen, nor ear heard, neither have entered into the heart of man, the things which God hath prepared for them that love him."* (1 Cor 2:9)

Walking in love literally means living our life, like Christ Jesus. It is a way for us to demonstrate our Love for God and for humanity. Every time you *walk in love* you *walk in God*. Apostle Paul asked a familiar question... *"Who shall separate us from the love of Christ? shall tribulation, or distress, or persecution, or famine, or nakedness, or peril, or sword?"* **Romans 8:35**

It is my prayer, that this small book will encourage you to live in peace with the love of God. May you live in kindness and love with all that God will send your way in Jesus Name.

Happy reading

HIS DESTINY WAS THE

CROSS....

HIS PURPOSE WAS

LOVE.....

HIS REASON WAS

YOU....

There is no fear in love; but perfect love casteth out fear:because fear hath torment. He that feareth is not made perfect in love.

1 John 4:18

Jesus said unto him, Thou shalt love the Lord thy God with all thy heart, and with all thy soul, and with all thy mind.

Matthew 22:37

This is the first and great commandment. And the second is like unto it, Thou shalt love thy neighbour as thyself. On these two commandments hang all the law and the prophets.

Matthew 22:38-40

PRAYER POINTS

*"If ye shall ask any thing in my name,
I will do it.."*
John 14:14

Holy Spirit of God frustrate and disappoint, every one that is against my life and family, in the name of Jesus.

Father Lord destroy every demonic networks and traps against my progress in life in the name of Jesus.

Fire of God, destroy every demonic projection and curses against my life and destiny in the name of Jesus.

Every spell and curses pronounced against my destiny, break, in the name of Jesus.

Hand of God cage every power militating against my rising in life, in the name of Jesus.

Power of God silent every voice raising a counter motion against my elevation, in the mighty name of Jesus.

Blood of Jesus neutralize every spirit of Balaam hired to hinder my life, ministry, and career, the name of Jesus.

Fire of God destroy every curse that I have brought into my life through ignorance and disobedience, break by fire, in the name of Jesus.

Ancient of day destroy every power harassing my ministry in the name of Jesus.

Father God deliver me from invincible forces militating against my life and destiny.

Power of God frustrate every coven and demonic network, designed to frustrate and hinder my success in life, in the name of Jesus.

I dismantle every strong hold designed to imprison my talent in the mighty name of Jesus.

I reject every cycle of frustration, in the name of Jesus.

Power of God paralyze every agent assigned to frustrate my life in the name of Jesus.

Finger of God, grant me supernatural speed against all my contenders in the name of Jesus.

By the blood of Jesus, I destroy every familiar spirit caging my life and career.

Fire of God arrest every demonic agents, assigned to police my destiny and marriage.

By the blood of Jesus, I proclaim no weapon fashioned against me shall ever prosper.

Holy Spirit of God break me through and forward in life in the mighty name of Jesus.

God, smash me and renew my strength, in the name of Jesus.

Holy Spirit, open my eyes to see beyond the visible to the invisible, in the name of Jesus.

Father Lord grant me strength and power in the name of Jesus

O Lord, liberate my spirit to follow the leading of the Holy Spirit.

Holy Spirit, teach me to pray through problems instead of praying about, it in the name of Jesus.

Father Lord, deliver me from the false accusation in life, in the name of Jesus

By the blood of Jesus, every evil spiritual padlock and evil chain hindering my success, be roasted, in the name of Jesus.

By the blood of Jesus I rebuke every spirit of spiritual deafness and blindness in my life, in the name of Jesus.

Father Lord, empower me to dominate the enemy of my destiny in the name of Jesus.

Jesus Christ of Nazareth, heal my infirmities in the name of Jesus

Lord, anoint my eyes and my ears that they may see and hear wondrous things from heaven.

Father Lord, anoint me with power and authority to dominate all my enemies in the name of Jesus.

Fire of God roast every giant rising up against my life and career.

Holy Spirit of God destroy all my oppressors in the name of Jesus.

Angels of good new, bring my good news to me in the mighty name of Jesus.

Every strong man holding me down, lose your hold now in the name of Jesus.

I nullify every demonic prediction over my life in the name of Jesus.

By the blood of Jesus, I flush out every polluted deposit of the enemy in my life.

By the blood of Jesus, I paralyze every enemy of my promotion in the name of Jesus.

Father Lord, destroy any power tormenting my life that is not from you.

Holy Ghost fire, ignite the fire of revival in my life.

By the blood of Jesus, I declare victory over every conflicting trial

By the Blood of Jesus, I command the arrest of every demonic spirit, militating against my life

By the blood of Jesus, I proclaimed the blood of Jesus, over every device of the enemy.

By the blood of Jesus, I revoke stagnation and hardship over my life in the name of Jesus.

Holy Ghost fire, destroy every satanic arrangement in my life, in the name of Jesus.

CHAPTER 1

WHAT IS LOVE?

"For God so loved the world that he gave his only begotten Son, that whosoever believeth in him should not perish, but have everlasting life."
John 3:16

In my own simple definition, *"God is love."* Every time *"you walk in love, you walk in God."* Although it is incomplete, when folks define love as *a mixture of different feelings, states, and attitudes that ranges from interpersonal affection to pleasure.* Again, *it is incomplete when some people refer love only, as a strong emotion or feeling of carnal attraction attached to pleasure or material gains.* In my own opinion every celebrated *"lover is a giver."* We are also told by the Holy Bible that *"perfect love cast out fear."*

The love of God is selfless and contended mind. Love is the Cost of Giving. Genuine love is a function of sacrifice. It is inevitable for selfish and self-centered people to genuinely prove the Love of God from the heart. *You can give without loving, but you can never love without giving.* In my opinion, genuine love is costly and it comes at a sacrificial cost. David said, *"....Neither will I offer burnt offerings unto the Lord my God of that which doth cost me nothing."* 2 Samuel 24:24

It is written, *"And we have known and believed the love that God hath to us. God is love; and he that dwelleth in love dwelleth in God, and God in him."* 1 John 4:16

The truth is, genuine *love of God* comes from the heart, but by the *grace of God*. It is not an impulse from feelings. *Love* can only be understood from the actions it prompts. It is written, *"And hope maketh not ashamed; because the love of God is shed abroad in our hearts by the Holy Ghost which is given unto us."* Romans 5:5

Anyone that claims to love God without proof is fake. Every time you genuinely walk in love it generates tangible result. Anyone that genuinely love God keep His commandment. *"He that hath my commandments, and keepeth them, he it is that loveth me: and he that loveth me shall be loved of my Father, and I will love him, and will manifest myself to him."* John 14:21

In my opinion the genuine love of God is inseparable. It is written, *"Who shall separate us from the love of Christ? shall tribulation, or distress, or persecution, or famine, or nakedness, or peril, or sword?"* Romans 8:35

How do I prove that I love God?

In my own opinion, it is incorrect to say *"love is God."* God created love, not the other way around. God willingly chose to make us in His image -- *revealing His very loving and compassionate nature inside of our heart.* It is written, *"I have said, Ye are gods; and all of you are children of the most High."* Psalms 82:6

It is written, *"And God said, Let us make man in our image, after our likeness: and let them have dominion over the fish of the sea, and over the fowl of the air, and over the cattle, and over all the earth, and over every creeping thing that creepeth upon the earth."* Genesis 1:26

Most of us live selfishly as a lifestyle. We live in *bitterness*, in *envy*, and in *strive*. The *love* of God is *kindness*, and *compassion*. It does not retain bitter memories, resentment, envy, or malice. It is written, *"Love is patient, love is kind. It does not envy, it does not boast, it is not proud. It does not dishonor others, it is not self-seeking, it is not easily angered, it keeps no record of wrongs. Love does not delight in evil but rejoices with the truth. It always protects, always trusts, always hopes, always perseveres. Love never fails."* 1 Cor 13:4-8

It is written, *"We know that we have passed from death unto life, because we love the brethren. He that loveth not his brother abideth in death. Whosoever hateth his brother is a murderer: and ye know that no murderer hath eternal life abiding in him. Hereby perceive we the love of God, because he laid down his life for us: and we ought to lay down our lives for the brethren. But whoso hath this world's good, and seeth his brother have need, and shutteth up his bowels of compassion from him, how dwelleth the love of God in him? My little children, let us not love in word, neither in tongue; but in deed and in truth."* 1 John 3:14-18

"All through the life, and ministry of Jesus Christ, it was recorded that He was a *compassionate* man. It is written, "When the Lord saw her, He felt compassion for her, and said to her, "Do not weep." (Luke 7:13) Furthermore also at a wedding in Canaan, we recorded that Jesus performed His first miracle out of *love*, and *compassion*. Often we all forget "It is of the Lord's mercies that we are not consumed, because his compassions fail not. They are new every morning: great is thy faithfulness." Lamentation 3:22-23

How Do I Walk In Love?

If you are walking in love, you must embrace righteousness, peace, and the love of God. Unless your heart is pure, you have no opportunity to walk in love. Unless you are living a righteous life, you have no chance to walk in love. Anyone living in regret, bitter, envious, jealous, and contentious, in strive, have no chance to walk in love.

The Almighty God want us to be humble, forgiving in life, compassionate and care for one another. It is written, "Jesus said unto him, Thou shalt love the Lord thy God with all thy heart, and with all thy soul, and with all thy mind. This is the first and great commandment. And the second is like unto it, Thou shalt love thy neighbor as thyself." Matthew 22:37-39

Unless we embrace *the Love of God from our heart*, it will be tough *for us to love anyone*. Unless we God and know God personally, the love of God cannot manifest upon our lifestyle. It is written, "He that hath my commandments, and keepeth them, he it is that loveth me: and he that loveth me shall be loved of my Father, and I will love him, and will manifest myself to him." John 14:21

No man can give what they do not have. It is easy for anyone to share what they have. It is written, *"Every man according as he purposeth in his heart, so let him give."* (2 Cor 9:7) One of the primary reason Jesus came was to establish a loving relationship between us and the Father. "We love him, because he first loved us." 1 John 4:19

Jesus shed His blood, so that *we may love*

him from our heart "...because the love of God is shed abroad in our hearts by the Holy Ghost which is given unto us." (Romans 5:5) Often most folks claim that they love God, but failed to manifest the love of God in their character and lifestyle. *"If a man say, I love God, and hateth his brother, he is a liar: for he that loveth not his brother whom he hath seen, how can he love God whom he hath not seen."* 1 John 4:20

Remember....

John answered and said, "A man can receive nothing, except it be given him from heaven." (John 3:27) God gave us the natural ability to show love, and to beloved. For the most part, except the Lord gives us the grace to love and beloved, what we call love is not the love of God. "For without me ye can do nothing." (John 15:5) The love of God has been sprinkled into our hearts by the Holy Spirit. We cannot continue to live in wickedness, pride, cynicism, anger, selfishness, and unbelief. Often most wicked people do not premeditate what they do. They just do it because they lack the consciousness of the love of God.

For us to *walk in love*, we must believe that "God is a rewarder, of those who diligently seek Him." Hebrews 11:6

We must embrace the lifestyle to depend on God at all times. This makes us appear faithful before Him. Every time you are faithful before Him, He becomes your companion. But we need to meet God in prayers, in supplication and in meditation on the Word of God. Our love for God and the Kingdom of God manifests when we spend time with God, in prayers, and in thanksgiving. Jesus said that the things we do for others we are doing to Him. It is written, *"He that hath pity upon the poor lendeth unto the Lord; and that which he hath given will he pay him again."* (Proverb 19:17) He that giveth unto the poor shall not lack: but he that hideth his eyes shall have many a curse. Proverb 28:27

We must to celebrate the love of God in our families. Love can be expressed in numerous ways. *Two very important ways that we can show the love of God is through words of affirmation, and through acts of service.* Words of affirmation can rekindle hope and confidence in a person who has suffered blows in life.

It is written, *"For God so loved the world that he gave his only begotten Son, that whosoever believeth in him should not perish, but have everlasting life."* John 3:16

Often we miss *the mystery of this dynamics of love,* when we read that "God is Love". But fail to apply this mystery into our daily lives. It is written, *"And we have known and believed the love that God hath to us. God is love; and he that dwelleth in love dwelleth in God, and God in him."* 1 John 4:16

This love is agape, it is selfless, divine, and compassionate in nature. Jesus Christ instructed us with the great commandment. It is written, **"Jesus said unto him, Thou shalt love the Lord thy God with all thy heart, and with all thy soul, and with all thy mind. This is the first and great commandment. And the second is like unto it, Thou shalt love thy neighbour as thyself."** Matthew 22:37-39

If we can take a minute and reflect about the life of Jesus Christ, who knew no sin, yet became the pass over lamb. Jesus laid down his life us for all. It is written "For God so loved the world that he gave his only begotten Son, that whosoever believeth in him should not perish, but have everlasting life." John 3:16

It is written, *"Greater love hath no man than this, that a man lay down his life for his friends."* John 15:13

PERFECT LOVE CAST OUT FEAR

It is written, "There is no fear in love; but perfect love casteth out fear: because fear hath torment. He that feareth is not made perfect in love." (1 John 4:18) Every time we walk in love we walk in boldness and authority, for we were told that perfect love cast out fear. Every time you walk in the devil cannot torment you. *The bible said, "The wicked flee when no man pursueth: but the righteous are bold as a lion."*

But to walk in love we must first recognize that He first love us. *"We love him, because he first loved us."* (1 John 4:19) Therefore if anyone must walk in love we must love everyone around us including our brothers and sister. It is written, "If a man say, I love God, and hateth his brother, he is a liar: for he that loveth not his brother whom he hath seen, how can he love God whom he hath not seen? And this commandment have we from him, That he who loveth God love his brother also." 1 John 4:20-21

CHAPTER 2

HOW DO I WALK IN LOVE?

"But as it is written, Eye hath not seen, nor ear heard, neither have entered into the heart of man, the things which God hath prepared for them that love him."
1 Cor 2:9

We all claim to know that familiar passage of the scripture where the bible said *"God is love."* Often most people *think of Love* as the celebration of an intimate relationship. Off course any intimate relationship must be *celebrated in love*. In my own little understanding, perfect love cast out fear, we were told by the Holy bible. Every *genuine lover is a celebrated giver in life*. Consider King Solomon for a second. It is written, *"And Solomon loved the Lord, walking in the statutes of David his father: only he sacrificed and burnt incense in high places. And the king went to Gibeon to sacrifice there; for that was the great high place: a thousand burnt offerings did Solomon offer upon that altar."* 1 King 3:3-4

To walk in love, means to *become a selfless celebrated giver.* To *walk in love means to live in peace with all men.* It is written, "Follow peace with all men, and holiness, without which no man shall see the Lord." (Hebrews 12:14) Anyone who lives in regret, and with bitter memories, does not love God. Anyone who is envy, jealous, proud, arrogant, vindictive does not know God, and is not walking in love. *God is love, that is His nature. If you cannot love, you do not know God, for no one cannot understands the deep mysteries of God without genuine love from the heart.* "He that loveth not knoweth not God; for God is love." 1 John 4:8

It is so important that we practice love in our daily lives. Often most folks claim they love but lack the evidence. Our lives will be more productive if we practice what we hear, and preach. For the most part our carnal nature is a big hindrance from celebrating the love of God with everyone around us. It is written, "Because the carnal mind is enmity against God: for it is not subject to the law of God, neither indeed can be. So then they that are in the flesh cannot please God." Romans 8:7-8

In my own opinion the word *love* is a moving word. It generates attention, and therefore requires immediate action. Love requires action. It's not something we purchase, rather we pay for love. Love is the action we express to others through sharing, and service. We prove our love for God by our giving and in obedience to His word. Often our pets are loyal to us because love and care for them. No one can obey a stranger. It is easy to obey someone that I know or that I am related to.

When Jesus talked about the greatest commandment of all, He quoted Deuteronomy 6:5 and said we are to love God with all our heart. But He also added the second greatest commandment: You shall love your neighbor as yourself. (See Mark 12:31) We all need to accept ourselves, embrace our personalities and even our imperfections, knowing that although we are not where we need to be, we are making progress. Jesus died for us because we have weaknesses and imperfections, and we don't have to reject ourselves because of them. God wants us to love ourselves and enjoy how He's made us!

We know that we have passed over out of death into Life by the fact that we love the brethren (our fellow Christians). He who does not love abides (remains, is held and kept continually) in [spiritual] death (1 John 3:14). Life, in this verse, is the life of God or "life as God has it." I don't want to be one of what I call "the walking dead"—someone who lives and breathes but never truly lives as God desires.

Loving others is the only way to keep the God-kind of life flowing through you. God's love is a gift to us; it's in us, but we need to release it to others through words and actions. Left dormant, it will stagnate like a pool of water with no outlet.

The act of loving others is one of the

most exhilarating things I have experienced. I feel excitement stirring in my spirit and soul when I plan to do something to make someone else feel loved and cared for. You can experience the same exhilaration just by "loving out loud." Here's a challenge: Think of three people you know who could really use a gesture of God's love. Then think of creative ways you can express His love to these people, and do it. I guarantee you will feel a wonderful sense of fulfillment and joy afterward.

CONCLUSION

"He that hath my commandments, and keepeth them, he it is that loveth me: and he that loveth me shall be loved of my Father, and I will love him, and will manifest myself to him." John 14:21

It is my desire through this small book for anyone reading to walk in love the remaining days of their lives. We live in a world and a time full of hate and evil, but as believer we must reflect the very nature of our God. It is written, "And we have known and believed the love that God hath to us. God is love; and he that dwelleth in love dwelleth in God, and God in him." 1 John 4:16

I pray this small book to help you remember the poor, the orphans, the destitute and prostitutes, the bereaved, all beggars and all the homeless and hopeless in life. May the Lord touch our heart with compassion and love.

What must I do to determine my divine visitation?

To determine divine visitation you must be born again! The word says as many as received him, to them gave He power to become the sons of God. Even to them that believe on his name.

To qualify for divine visitation, do the following with sincerity—

1) Acknowledge that you are a sinner and that He died for you. (Romans 3:23)

2) Repent of your sins. (Acts 3:19, Luke 13:5, 2 Peter 3:9)

3) Believe in your heart that Jesus died for your sin. (Romans 10:10)

4) Confess Jesus as the Lord over your life. (Romans 10:10, Acts 2:21)

Now repeat this Prayer after me

Say Lord Jesus, I accept you today, as my Lord and my savior, forgive me of my sins wash me with your blood. Right now, I believe, I am sanctified, I am save, I am free, I am free from the Power of sin to serve the Lord Jesus. Thank you Lord for saving me. Amen.

Congratulations: You are now...

A BORN AGAIN CHRISTIAN.
Again I say to you—

CONGRATULATIONS!

I dare you to watch the Spirit of God bear witness with your Spirit confirming His word with signs following. The word says The Spirit itself beareth witness with our spirit, that we are the children of God. Join a bible believing church or join us on our weekly and Sunday worship services at 343 Sanford Avenue, Newark, New Jersey, 07106.

WISDOM KEYS

— Every Productive Society is a society heading to the top.

— Millions of Nigerians run away from Nigeria, very few Nigerians stay in Nigeria.

— My decision to return Nigeria is the will of God for my life.

— My short coming in America after 18 years, trained me to be wise, to think, reflect and reason appropriately.

— If you train your mind to reason it will train your hands to earn money.

— It is absurd to use the money of the heathen to build the kingdom of the living God.

— Every Ministry reveals its agenda and goal either at the beginning or at the end. Be careful of your life it is your first Ministry.

— The average American mind is conditioned for a continual quest to get new things and (discard the former) and throw away old things.

— When I considered well, my BMW jeep became my initial deposit for the work of the ministry in Nigeria.

— Money will never fall from any tree.

— Everyone is waiting for you to change your mind until you change your thinking nothing changes around you.

— Multiple academic degrees in other discipline gave me the chance to think, reflect and reason.

— What so everyone are thinking and reflecting at the moment reveals you to the time and the now factor.

— All events and intents are the product of precise thought processes, accurate reason every event is designed for a designated timeline.

— Wisdom is your ability to think, to create and invent. If you can think wise enough you will come out of penury.

— The distance between you and success is your creative ability to think reason and reflect accurate.

— Success is the result of hard work, commitment resolve and determination learning from past mistakes and failing.

— If you organize your mind you have organized your life and destiny.

— There is a thin line between success and failure. If you look above and beyond you are on your way to success.

— Wealth is your ability to think, power is your ability to reason and success is your ability to be informed.

— If you can make use of your mind by thinking and reasoning God will make use of your life and destiny.

— Think and Be Great.

— Reflect, Reason, Think and Be Great.

— Famous people are born of woman.

— That you will make it is your intention; that you will survive is your resolve, that you will succeed with changes is your determination, personal efforts and hard work.

— No man was born a failure. Lack of vision is the end product of failure.

— Working with mental patients encourages and aspire me to be a productive observant and dedicated to my assignment.

— Successful people are not magicians, it is the will power combined with hard work, and determination and a resolve to succeed that make them succeed.

— In the unequivocal state of the mind, intention is not a location or a position it is the state of the mind.

— So many people think, that they think. The mind is used to think, reflect, and reason. You will remain blind with your eye open until you can see with your mind by thinking.

— There is no favoritism in accurate and precise calculation.

— Although knowledge is power, information is the key and gateway to a great future.

— It will take the hand of God to move the hand of man.

— With the backing of the great wise God, nothing will disconnect you from your inheritance.

— As long as you have wisdom and understanding of God, Satan and evil cannot manipulate your life and destiny.

— You have come this far by yourself judgment and decision you have made in the past, now lean and listen to God for another dimension of greatness.

— Great people are common people it is extra ordinary effort and the price of sacrifice that produces greatness.

— As a mental direct care worker I saw a great pastor and a motivational speaker within myself.

— Menial job does not reduce your self-worth, until you resolve to achieve greatness see greatness in all you do; you will never count in your community.

— The principle of Jesus will solve your gambling and addiction problems.

— The man of Jesus will lead you into heaven.

— Everyone have their self-appraisal and what they think about you. Until you discover yourself other opinion about you will alter the real you.

— Supervisors and directors are just a position in the chain of command in a work place. Never allow your supervisor hierarchy to alter your opinion about yourself.

— Everyone can come out of debt if they make up their mind.

— That I am not a decision maker at work does not diminish my contribution to my world.

— Although it appears like it was a poor decision to accept a direct care employment at a psychiatric hospital as I reflect of my nine years of experience, it became apparent that I have learnt and experienced enough for my next assignment in life.

— Self-encouragement and determination is a resolve of the heart.

— If you are determined to make a difference, and do the things that make a difference you will eventually make a difference.

— Good things do not come easy.

— Short cuts will cut your life short.

— Those who look ahead move ahead.

— Life is all about making an impact. In your life time strive to make an impact in your community.

— Make friends and connect with people who are moving ahead of you in life.

— If you can look around well you have come a long way in your life, made a lot of difference and realized a lot of success in life.

— If you are my old friend, hurry up to reach out to me before I become a stranger to you.

— Everything I am blessed with inspirations from God, that change my definition and interpretation of the world around me.

— I thought I was stagnant and lonely until I looked around and noticed my children running around and my wife cooking.

— At 40 I resigned my Job to seek the Lord forever.

— My ministry took a drastic rise to the top when the wisdom of God visited me with knowledge and understanding.

— You will be a better person, if you understand the characteristics of your personality – your mood swings, attitudes, and habits.

— It is the seed of love you sow into the heart of a child and a woman that you reap in due time.

— Love is not selfish, love share everything including the concealed secrets of the mind.

— As long as you have a prayer life and a bible; you will never feel lonely, rejected, and idle in the race of life.

— When good friends disconnect from you, let them go, they might have seen something new in a different direction.

— Confidence in yourself and in God is the only way to bring you out of captivity.

— Never train a child to waste his/her time.

— The mind is the greatest assets of a great future.

— You walk by common sense run by principles and fly by instruction.

— Those who fly in flight of life fly alone.

— Up in the air you are alone. No one can toll you accept the compass of knowledge and information.

— I have seen a towing vehicle I have seen a towing ship I have never seen a tolling airplane.

— I exercise my judgment and make a decision every minute of the day.

— Decisions are crucial, critical and vital with reference to your future.

— So many people wish for a great future. You can only work towards a great future.

— Your celebrity status began when you discovered your talent. What are you good at? Work at it with all commitment.

— Prayers will sustain you but the wisdom of God will prosper you.

— When I met Oyedepo, his teachings changed my perspective. But when I met Ibiyeomie; His teaching changed my perception.

— I will be successful in ministry if only I concentrate and focus my energy in the work of the ministry.

— It took the late Dr. Vincent Pearle Norman's book to open my mind towards kingdom success.

CHAPTER 3

PRAYER OF SALVATION

"Neither is there salvation in any other: for there is none other name under heaven given among men, whereby we must be saved."
Acts 4:12

What must I do to determine my salvation?

To be saved we must be born again! The word says as many as received him, to them gave He power to become the sons of God. Even to them that believe on his name.

To qualify for divine visitation, do the following with sincerity—

1) Acknowledge that you are a sinner and that He died for you. (Romans 3:23)

2) Repent of your sins. (Acts 3:19, Luke 13:5, 2 Peter 3:9)

3) Believe in your heart that Jesus died for your sin. (Romans 10:10)

4) Confess Jesus as the Lord over your life. (Romans 10:10, Acts 2:21)

Now repeat this Prayer after me

Say Lord Jesus, I accept you today, as my Lord and my savior, forgive me of my sins wash me with your blood. Right now, I believe, I am sanctified, I am save, I am free, I am free from the Power of sin to serve the Lord Jesus. Thank you Lord for saving me. Amen.

Congratulations: You are now...

A BORN AGAIN CHRISTIAN.
Again I say to you—

CONGRATULATIONS!

I adjure you to watch the Spirit of God bear witness with your Spirit confirming His word with signs following. The word says The Spirit itself beareth witness with our spirit, that we are the children of God.

MIRACLE CARE OUTREACH

"...But that the members should have the same care one for another"
1 Corinthians 12:25

We are all members of the body of Christ. Jesus commanded us to love our neighbor as ourselves. This includes caring for one another as a member of one body. True love is expressed in caring and giving. The word says for God so Love He gave….

Reach out to someone in need of Jesus, help someone in crisis find Christ. Look out and prove your love to Jesus by caring and inviting your friends and associates to find Jesus the Healer.

Invite your friends to our Home Care Cell Fellowship (Miracle chapel Intl Satellite fellowship) In the USA at 33 Schley Street, Newark, New Jersey, 07112. Home Care Cell fellowship Group meets every Tuesday at 6:00pm-7:00pm.

If you are in Nigeria—**MIRACLE OF GOD MINISTRIES**, aka "**MIRACLE CHAPEL INTL**" Mpama –Egbu-Owerri Imo state Nigeria.

LIFE IS NOT ALL ABOUT DURATION—
BUT ITS ALL ABOUT DONATION

What does the above statement mean?....

Life consists not in the accumulation of material wealth. (Luke 12:15) But it's all about liberality...meaning - what you can give and share with others. Proverb11:25. When you live for others—You live forever - because you out live your generation by the legacy you live behind after you depart into glory to be with the Lord. But when you live to yourself - you are reduced to self—you are easily forgotten when you die and depart in glory. Permit me to admonish you today to live your life to be a blessing to a soul connected to you today. I want you to know that so many souls are connected and looking up to you, and through you so many souls will be saved and rescued from destruction. Will you disciple someone today to find Jesus Christ?

As a genuine Christian; it is your duty to evangelize Jesus Christ to all you meet on your way. Jesus is still in the healing business-Jesus is still doing miracles from time of old to now. Therefore tell someone about Jesus Christ today, disciple and bring them to Church. (John 1:45) Philip findeth Nathanael....

Please to prove the sincerity of your love for God today; please become a soul winner. The dignity of your Christianity is hidden in your boldness to proclaim and evangelize Jesus Christ to all you meet on your way. There is a question mark on the integrity of your Christianity until you become a life soul winner. Invite someone to join us worship the Lord Jesus this coming Sunday. Amen.

MIRACLE OF GOD MINISTRIES

PILLARS OF THE COMMISSION

We Believe Preach and Practice the following:

1) We believe and preach Salvation to every living human being

2) We believe and preach Repentance and forgiveness of sins

3) We believe and preach the baptism of the Holy Spirit and Spiritual gifts

4) We believe and teach the Prosperity

5) We believe and preach Divine Healing and Miracles (Signs & Wonder)

6) We believe and preach Faith

7) We believe and proclaim the Power of God (Supernatural)

8) We believe and proclaim Praise & Worship to God

9) We believe and preach Wisdom

10) We believe and preach Holiness (Consecration)

11) We believe and preach Vision

12) We believe and teach the Word of God

13) We believe and teach Success

14) We believe and practice Prayer

15) We believe and teach Deliverance

These 15 stones form the Pillars of Our Commission. Become part of this church family and follow this great move of God.

MY HEART FELT PRAYER FOR YOU

It is my prayer that you testify today about the goodness of the Lord. I desire for you to have an encounter with our Lord Jesus Christ.

Now let me pray for you:

Heavenly father may today be a day of new beginning for this precious love one. Lord God of heaven, you love us, may we love you back genuinely from the heart in the mighty Name of Jesus. Father Lord shower us with your infinite mercy and love as it is written.

WHAT TO DO WHEN MIRACLE SEEMS TO BE DELAYED:

1) Praise God even in times of trouble, trial, and tribulations.

2) Be expectant- expect God to move beyond imagination.

3) Be willing and Obedient-God look at your obedient in times of delay.

4) Be focus—God expect us to pay relevant attention to details.

5) Do not quit- If we must emerge winners, quitting is not an option.

6) Be positive—it can only get better so be positive.

7) Be optimistic--- Your case is different so be optimistic in life.

8) Develop all possibility mentality—Every limitation is within you faith.

PROVE YOUR LOVE FOR GOD BY YOUR GIVING

Often we claim we love God with our mouth, how many of us can prove the sincerity of our love for Christ Jesus. We musts embrace integrity of the heart with genuine love for God and His Kingdom, if we claim we live in love. We must learn to pray as often as possible. The Altar of prayer is the altar of sacrifice. For unless you lay it all on the Altar you make your love for Him fake. It is written "No man taketh it from me, but I lay it down of myself. I have power to lay it down, and I have power to take it again. This commandment have I received of my Father." John 10:18

King Solomon loved the Lord and gave. It is written "And Solomon loved the Lord, walking in the statutes of David his father: only he sacrificed and burnt incense in high places. And the king went to Gibeon to sacrifice there; for that was the great high place: a thousand burnt offerings did Solomon offer upon that altar." 1 King 3:3-4

For God so loved the world that he gave.... It is written, "For God so loved the world that he gave his only begotten Son, that whosoever believeth in him should not perish, but have everlasting life." John 3:16

Every lover must become a celebrated giver in life. Every lover must be willing to give and sacrifice their time, talent, and money.

CHAPTER 4

ABOUT THE AUTHOR

Rev Franklin N Abazie is the founding and Presiding Pastor of Miracle of God Ministries with headquarters in Newark, New Jersey USA and a branch church in Owerri- Imo State Nigeria. He is following the footsteps of one of his mentors, Oral Roberts (Healing Evangelist) of the blessed memory. The Lord passed Oral Roberts healing mantle two days before he went to be with the Lord at age 91 into the hand of healing evangelist-Rev Franklin N Abazie in a vision.

In all his services the Power and Presence of God is present to heal all in his audience. He is an ordained man of God with a Healing Ministry reviving the healing and miracle ministry of Jesus Christ of Nazareth.

Pastor Franklin N Abazie, is called by God with a unique mandate: **"THE MOMENT IS DUE TO IMPACT YOUR WORLD THROUGH THE REVIVAL OF THE HEALING & MIRACLE MINISTRY OF JESUS CHRIST OF NAZARETH**

"I AM SENDING YOU TO RESTORE HEALTH UNTO THEE AND I WILL HEAL

THEE OF THY WOUNDS. SAID THE LORD OF HOST"

Rev. Abazie is a gifted ardent Teacher of the word of God who operates also in the office of a Prophet, generating and attracting undeniable signs & wonders, special miracles and healings, with apostolic fireworks of the Holy Ghost. He is the founding and presiding senior Pastor of this fast growing Healing ministry. He has written over 86 inspirational, healing and transforming books covering almost all aspect of divine healing and life. He is happily married and blessed with children.

BOOKS BY REV FRANKLIN N ABAZIE

1) The Outcome of Faith
2) Understanding the secret of prevailing Prayers
3) Commanding Abundance
4) Understanding the secret of the man God uses
5) Activating my due Season
6) Overcoming Divine Verdicts
7) The Outcome of Divine Wisdom
8) Understanding God's Restoration Mandate
9) Walking in the Victory and Authority of the truth
10) Gods Covenant Exemption
11) Destiny Restoration Pillars
12) Provoking Acceptable Praise
13) Understanding Divine Judgment
14) Activating Angelic Re-enforcement
15) Provoking Un-Merited Favor
16) The Benefits of the Speaking faith
17) Understanding Divine Arrangement
18) Put your faith to work
19) Developing a positive attitude in life
20) The Power of Prevailing faith
21) Inexplicable faith
22) The intellectual components of Redemption.
23) Dominating Controlling Spirit
24) Understanding Divine Prosperity
25) Understanding the secret of the man God Uses
26) Retaining Your Inheritance
27) Never give up hope
28) Commanding Angelic Escorts
29) The winner's faith
30) Understanding Your Guardian Angels
31) Overcoming the Dominion of Sin
32) Understanding the Voice of God

33) The Outstanding benefits of the Anointing
34) The Audacity of the Blood of Jesus
35) Walking in the Reality of the Anointing
36) The Mystery of Divine supply
37) Understanding Your Harvest Season
38) Activating Your Success Buttons
39) Overcoming the forces of Darkness
40) Overcoming the devices of the devil
41) Overcoming Demonic agents
42) Overcoming the sorrows of failure
43) Rejecting the Sorrows of failure
44) Resisting the Sorrows of Poverty
45) The Restoring broken Marriages.
46) Redeeming Your Days
47) The force of Vision
48) Overcoming the forces of ignorance
49) Understanding the sacrifice of small beginning
50) The might of small beginning
51) Praying in the Spirit
52) Dominating controlling Spirits
53) Breaking the shackles of the curse of the law
54) Covenant keys to answered prayers
55) Wisdom for Signs & Wonders
56) Wisdom for generational Impact
57) Wisdom for Marriage Stability
58) Understanding the number of your Days
59) Enforcing Your Kingdom Rights
60) Escaping the traps of immoralities
61) Escaping the trap of Poverty
62) Accessing Biblical Prosperity
63) Accessing True Riches in Christ
64) Silencing the Voice of the Accuser
65) Overcoming the forces of oppositions
66) Quenching the voice of the avenger
67) Silencing demonic Prediction & Projection
68) Silencing Your Mocker

69) Understanding the Power of the Holy Ghost
70) Understanding the baptism of Power
71) The Mystery of the Blood of Jesus
72) Understanding the Mystery of Sanctification
73) Understanding the Power of Holiness
74) Praying in the spirit
75) Activating the Forces of Vengeance
76) Appreciating the Mystery of Restoration
77) Covenant Keys to Answered Prayers
78) Engaging the mystery of the blood
79) Commanding the Power of the Speaking faith
80) Uprooting the forces against Your Rising
81) Overcoming mere success syndrome
82) Understanding Divine Sentence
83) Understanding the Mystery of Praise
84) Understanding the Author of Faith
85) The Mystery of the finisher of faith
86) Where is your trust?

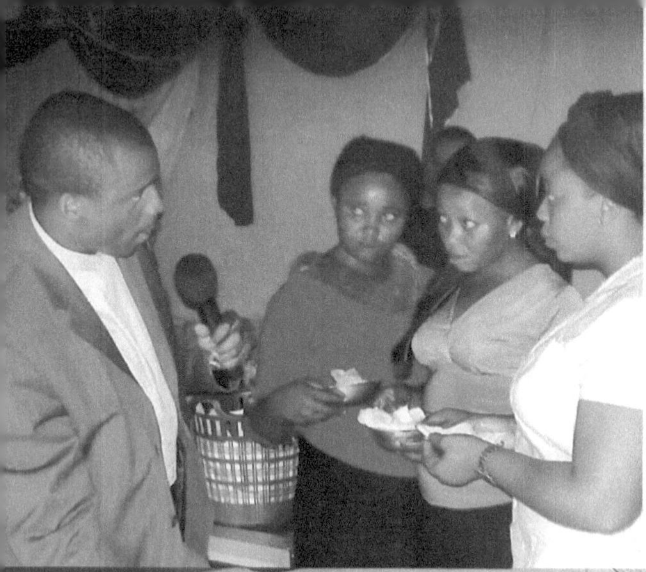

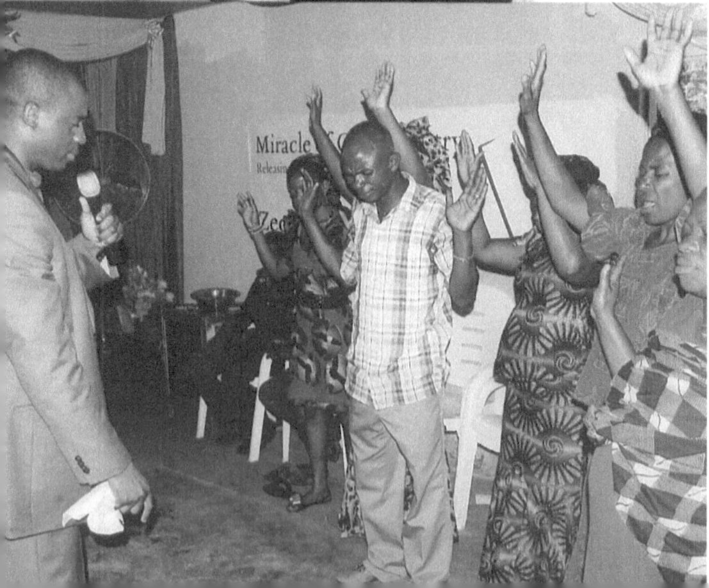
Miracle

MIRACLE OF GOD MINISTRIES

NIGERIA CRUSADE 2012

MIRACLE OF GOD MINISTRIES

NIGERIA CRUSADE 2012

MIRACLE OF GOD MINISTRIES

*NIGERIA CRUSADE
2012*

www.ingramcontent.com/pod-product-compliance
Lightning Source LLC
Chambersburg PA
CBHW021451080526
44588CB00009B/799